To

Portsmouth Public Library

By

THE SOLOMON B. FOSTER TRUST

Foster S. Goldman, Jr. Trustee

Spiritual Trails to Happiness

Solomon Foster

BOOKMAN ASSOCIATES
NEW YORK

First printing, 1953
Second printing, 1955
Third printing, second edition, 1957
Fourth printing, third edition, 1959
Fifth printing, third edition, 1962
Sixth printing, third edition, 1969
Seventh printing, third edition, 1974

PRINTED IN THE U.S.A.
BY FINANCIAL PRESS CORPORATION, PITTSBURGH

CONTENTS

I

THE ASSURANCES OF DIVINITY

THE TRAIL TO GOD

"Canst thou find out the deep things of God?"   Job 11:7

The trail that leads to God has many turns:
It climbs unto the mountain peaks by day
And nightly twists among the stars its way.
Deciphering the signs, the searcher learns
The path returns to earth. The trees and ferns,
The glories of the Master Mind display.
Perhaps the streams that fill the sea can say,
Where winds the blessed path for which man yearns.

Engirded with repose the mountain lends
And goals reflecting the celestial gleams
The eager searcher, like responsive streams,
Cheers lonely hearts and to the humble bends.
By blasting handicaps and social sins
He finds at last where trail to God begins.

THERE IS A GOD

"The fool hath said in his heart: 'There is no God' ".
Psalms 14:1

The flowers at my door present a code
That proves earth's kinship with infinity,
Ties human goals to cosmic unity,
And links the universe to my abode.
Its floral text, writ in a matchless mode,
Expounds in unexampled clarity
These three majestic symbols: G-O-D,
As Light which shines upon life's every road.

From gifts of God, our homes and souls are made;
He gives true love its highest ecstasy;
He charts each righteous cause to victory;
He heeds each fervent prayer that earns His aid.
With God, the true, the brave, the wise endure.
Without Him, waste and woe and war are sure.

THUS SAITH THE LORD

"And the Lord said: 'Shall I hide from Abraham that which I am doing, seeing that all the nations of the earth shall be blessed in him?'"

Genesis 18:17

"Through minds and hearts alert and souls awake,
　My treasury of nature and its lore,
　Writ large and luminous upon the core
　Of life, I offer to mankind. I make
　My deepest secrets known to those who take
　The risks of time and effort to explore
　My world. I give My still uncharted store
　Of wealth to all who can with falsehood break.

"Each spot on earth may still be holy ground,
　Where honest thinking and courageous deeds
　Prevail. An unrecorded moment needs
　Some worthy aim to fix a date profound.
　On prince or pauper, prophecy will fall
　The instant man makes ready for My call".

"HEAR, O ISRAEL"

"Ye are My witnesses, Saith the Lord."   Isaiah 43:10

Like gulf stream coursing through tumultuous seas
To temper sun and wind to nourish man,
A people wander 'round the globe with plan
To feed the soul and plant broad sympathies
In human hearts. With Heaven's wise decrees,
Defying bigot's shrieks and plots, they scan
With hope the darkness, since the world began
For dawn of day, when hate and war shall cease.

The earth is thine, with faith to make sublime,
O Israel. With courage thou must speak
God's truths, and fearlessly His justice seek
For all, as prelude to a peaceful time.
Fear not, O Israel, the tyrant's jeer,
While voice of the Eternal thou dost hear.

THE LIGHT OF THE NATIONS

"I will give thee for a light of the nations".   Isaiah 49:6

God made the sun to end the planet's night.
But for the darkness still within man's mind
He shaped a tiny lantern for mankind
And summoned Israel to bear the light
To kindle virtue, radiate the right,
To gladden the depressed and guide the blind
Along the only path in which to find
Security and life, serene and bright.

The bearer warns, but men refuse to heed.
The light is dim because the eyes of man
Are magnetized by glamour of a plan
That deepens the abyss of human greed.
The charge to guard the light will not be filled
Until the holy life men choose to build.

THE MAJESTY OF GOD

"Ascribe ye greatness unto God."   Deuteronomy 32:3

The ancients thought the same bright stars we see
Were supermen of Heaven. They were slow
To fathom that the planets which we know
Are globes of breathless speed and majesty.
The same old sea they viewed with tragedy
Shows us great order in its ebb and flow.
The same old earth which brought them endless woe
Means home to us and rich fertility.

The same old God the ancients held in dread,
Our Faith assures us is a God of Love,
Who links our life with all the stars above
And bids all nature aid us earn our bread.
God's greater majesty we will discern,
When laws and ways of Brotherhood we learn.

THE SANCTUARY

"Build Me a sanctuary."   Exodus 25:8

God's Presence dwells within this holy place:
His Spirit searching for an earthly home
Finds welcome underneath our friendly dome
Where vision and reality embrace.

Here earth and heaven merge within the scheme
Of cosmic unity. Here matter bends
To mind and worship generates the trends
To build an age from substance of a dream.

God meets with man whose life confirms the view
That self is merest shadow of the race,
The body but a fraction of all space,
And time a frame to fit the good and true.

Man meets with God when planets shrink in size
And gold appears like tinsel brightly hued,
When finite minds reflect infinitude
And love of God becomes earth's choicest prize.

Acceptance of God's will makes weak wills strong;
In atmosphere of truth sick souls are healed;
Sad hearts protected by religion's shield
Sing jubilantly life's triumphant song.

The Shrine bestows as its most precious gift
Man's wish and will and wisdom to unite
To make all hearts and souls alert to right
To further social good and world uplift.

The hidden strength by which man's conscience lives,
Creation's most enduring element,
The might of right and sway of sentiment
Are blessings only true religion gives.

When God's dear name upon man's pathway shines,
The soul discovers, with prophetic thrill,
How flower, wave, and star express His will
And stones are turned into the noblest Shrines.

The pure is permanent, all else is vain:
The loss of treasured clay man will not mourn,
The threats of brutal force he holds in scorn,
When faith in God and righteousness remain.

Faith ripens man for challenge of an age,
Shows ways by which the home and state endure,
Imparts to faithful souls the motives pure
That earn high place on history's bright page.

The only road that leads to human wealth
Is paved by Sinai's laws and hopes and ways;
To lose or leave this path for carefree days
Confuses man and blasts his commonwealth.

Contempt of vision vulgarizes man:
The gongue becomes a spear, the hand a claw
The mind a mere machine, without a law
To mold the years and life upon a plan.

If fate man would control and progress gain
The soul must find and keep God's Spirit near,
And to His warnings and commands give ear,
Till vice submits to virtue's endless reign.

To climb the highest peak of reason fair
And use the fruits of earth in happiness
The soul must march beyond the wilderness
To plan, construct, and love the House of Prayer.

THE MESSAGE OF YPSILON

"Thou mayest tell thy sons My signs which I have done
 among them."   Exodus 10:2

On face of Ypsilon a message clear
Is boldly sculptured, a gigantic "Y",
Suspended with a purpose from the sky
To give to drooping spirits needed cheer.
Eternal snows that fill the grooves appear
To make the letter seem to passer-by,
Just fastened on the rock to satisfy
His search for sign by which his life to steer.

The "Y" means *youth*, of few or many years
Who from the height can cast away all fears.
The "Y" spells *Yea* for lovers of the right
Who offer truth and honor all their might.
The "Y" is sign for "*Yanks*" who have unfurled
Old Glory as a blessing to the world.

THE HOUSE OF THE LORD

"Let us go to the House of the Lord."   Psalms 122:1

"I rejoiced when they said unto me,
 'Let us go to the House of the Lord,'"
And derive from its calm sanctity
The great good our devotions afford.

The routine of the week drives us mad,
With conflicting demands and pursuits.
We exchange precious hours for a fad
And pay dearly for poisonous fruits.

We are bound like a cog to a wheel
That keeps running to markets and sales,
Branding leisure with marks of a deal,
Filling dreams with quotations and scales.

Restless nights lead to feverish days
Overburdened with problems and snags.
Saturated with parties and plays
Our rich spiritual heritage sags.

To raise life high above the machine,
We must break the routine of our day
And appeal to the Father Unseen
To inspire us with yearning to pray.

We will earn what we need with less strife,
And donate larger gifts with more joy,
We will lead a far happier life,
If firm faith in the Lord we employ.

Faith turns scowls into smiles at our chores
And constructs out of crude drudgery
A fine house having wide open doors
Into service and self-mastery.

Without plan and a center of power,
The most casual claims right of way,
While an orbit and program each hour
Summon conscience and law into play.

Frictions melt, fancies lag, follies pall
When eternity enters the mind:
Factions fade, frenzies wane, fractions fall
When good-will unifies humankind.

Far less whimsical neighbors appear,
Carping critics show less cynicism
When our bearing grows gentle and clear
Under rays of a spiritual prism.

Our tomorrows through onrushing years,
Forming links with our life of today
Will know fewer distresses and fears,
If we follow the impulse to pray.

The soft beauty of flower and stream,
The bold grandeur of planet and hill
Radiate with an augmented gleam,
When discerned as expressing God's will.

From our past we inherit a trust
With which loyalists never would part.
We may turn it to-day into rust,
Unless truly we give it our heart.

Be ascribing all glory to God
Our own nature enhances its worth.
If with thanks we use gifts of the sod
We draw nearer God's Kingdom on earth.

THE JEWISH SOUL

"If I forget thee, O Jerusalem
  Let my right hand forget her cunning.
  Let my tongue cleave to the roof of my mouth,
  If I remember thee not".   Psalms 137:5

Jerusalem, my tongue shall ever praise
Thy soul. My hands, with all their strength and skill
Shall weave in living forms Jehovah's will,
Revealed to Zion's seers in ancient days.
For times like these, around the globe, I'll raise
In triumph Sinai's shining truths until
God's holy laws and inspirations fill
The hearts of men with fructifying rays.

The Jewish soul and not Judean soil
Determines Israel's true destiny:
To give the earth its only sanctity,
The fruit of Faith and sacrificial toil;
To lead mankind to the Prophetic goal,
ONE GOD, ONE WORLD, ONE UNIVERSAL SOUL.

THE AMERICAN

    The "A" means highest quality
    For what we know on earth is best:
A   Our freedom and democracy
    And happiness, by any test.

    The "MER" alludes to mighty sea,
M   A source of life and unity,
E   Like our dear country, strong and free,
R   America, best home for me.

    The "I" includes both you and me,
    Like all the brave of yesteryears,
I   To build defences that will be
    Safeguards of peace and future cheers.

    If life and fortune we must spend:
C   Can you respond to-day? I "CAN."
A   We can, we will, we must defend
N   The world's best name, AMERICAN.

    Our land, as proof of prophecy,
    With faith in God and our own soul,
    As clues to human destiny,
    We give mankind our highest goal.

U . . S . . A . .

Unity   Security   Aspiration

II

THE FOUNDATIONS OF HUMANITY

LOVE OF FELLOWMEN

"Thou shalt love thy neighbor as thyself."   Leviticus 19:18

The best in me invites the best in you
To join with all who know that destiny
Must guide us to a world fraternity.
The loyalties and goals that we pursue,
Our joys and pains, our friends and foes, are due
To our conceptions of humanity.
To reach the peak of personality,
To Brotherhood of Man each must be true.

In our associations do we live:
Our thoughts about the stars and streams, our health,
And every substance we transform to wealth
Derive from services our neighbors give.
To heed this law of human unity
Assures us peace and real security.

CHOOSE THE GOOD

"I call heaven and earth to witness against you this day, that
I have set before thee life and death, choose life, that thou
mayest live."   Deuteronomy 30:19

Each year that destiny allots to man
Bestows no blessing equal to the chance
To choose the good and honor to advance,
So that the whole of life reflect God's plan.

The years yield limitless monotony:
Sun-rise and evening star, like hidden streams
That vanish in the sea, are nameless gleams,
Unless they radiate Divinity.

The spirit in the wheels makes labor good,
And goals more than the goods interpret life;
Futility and folly follow strife,
But endless blessings flow from brotherhood.

The earth seems naught but unresponsive soil
Until the soul, with patient skill, by God
Assured, sows fertile faith into the sod
And shares with gratitude the boons of toil.

The lofty peaks and lovely trees we prize
Need contact with man's spirit to be real;
All life is vain and joy we cannot feel,
Until God's purpose we can recognize.

OUR COUNTRY IS HOLY GROUND

"The place whereon thou standeth is Holy Ground."

Exodus 3:5

America is more than wealth that lies
Imbedded in the earth; more than content
With fertile fields; more than the continent
That joins our seas and smiles at friendly skies.
America enfolds a plan that ties
Our nation's life and laws to sentiment,
To rights and principles for which men spent
Their blood for centuries to realize.

Our faith in freedom and democracy
Builds here the best defense of human rights
And kindles for all faiths their brightest lights.
In statesmanship and world philanthropy,
In peace and welfare for the common man,
God's favor shines on the American.

ABRAHAM LINCOLN

"And I heard the voice of the Lord, saying: 'Whom shall I
send?' Then I said: 'Here am I; send me'. And He said: 'Go,
and tell this people' ".   Isaiah 6:8

Unseen, but clearer than the highest peaks
On which time shines with timeless majesty;
Intangible, but real as memory
That blends the ages with the passing weeks,
The soul of Abraham Lincoln lives and speaks
To-day, from Springfield, to humanity
With limitless and vibrant verity,
Transpiercing global gloom with hopeful streaks.

The world cannot endure half-slave, half free;
The fictions by which blood and soil divide
The human house are falling, as the tide
Of freedom sweeps toward global unity.
The fight for brotherhood can never cease,
Until man earns a democratic peace.

THE BEGINNING OF A NEW ERA

"Lay not thy hand upon the lad, neither do thou anything unto him".
                                                    Genesis 22:12

A thousand years of evil reached an end,
The moment Abraham and Isaac sought
Moriah's peak, and a decision wrought
Which gave to history a nobler trend.
In human sacrifice the tribes made blend
Of fear and cruelty by which they thought
The aid of pagan godlings might be bought:
On misery and death such gods depend.

The crisis raged in Abraham's great soul:
Shall ancient rite retard evolving right?
Must moral strength be slave to brutal might?
A pioneer, he earned the hero's role:
To human sacrifice he put an end;
And turned the thoughts of men to God as Friend.

THE LEADERSHIP OF THE CHILD

"And a little child shall lead them."   Isaiah 11:6

Mankind must be as brave and free,
    As true and just as children are,
Whose spirits leap from out the deep
    To match the hopes of Morning Star.

When children wake, they truly make
    The sun shine with a brighter hue;
As lovely flowers grace the hours
    The calls of duty they renew.

When children play, life feels the sway
    Of rhythm, rhyme and jollity;
All thought of gloom, all fear of doom,
    Seem shadows of reality.

When children sing, eternal spring
    Spreads beauty o'er the hardened earth:
Vexations lift and sorrows shift,
    While troubles quickly turn to mirth.

When children learn to take the turn
    That leads to wisdom's safer ways,
They choose the deed that helps to speed
    To-morrow's nobler, brighter days.

When children love, there's naught above
    The happiness they generate
In hearts restrained, in minds enchained
    By greed and scorn, by fear and hate.

When children pray and mark their way
    With aims inspired by God's dear name,
They banish tears from later years,
    And guard their lives from sin and shame.

When children sleep, the wise must weep
    For human sins that blast their dreams,
For crimes that grieve and shams that leave
    To youth earth's pains and nature's seams.

As final truth, the needs of youth
    Must motivate each law and plan,
Till social good and brotherhood
    Enrich the common life of man.

THE PRICE OF HAPPINESS

"Happy is the man who hath not walked in the counsel of the
wicked, nor stood in the way of sinners, but his delight is in
the law of the Lord".   Psalms 1:1

A mansion gives no guarantee to fame;
No cabin ever cramps a soaring soul
That sets and seeks courageously some goal
Far distant from the scene from which it came.
In highest and in lowest ranks the same
Procedure rules and corresponding toll
Is paid for peace by all who play the role
That earns the richest prize in life's great game.

The range and depth of soul count more than speed
In limitless progression to the truth.
A social aim must sway both age and youth,
And dream more than the dreamer take the lead.
The heart much louder than the tongue must speak,
If human happiness we wisely seek.

III

THE SANCTITY OF PERSONALITY

VALIANT JEWISH WOMEN

"For their price is far above rubies."   Proverbs 31:10

God summons Wisdom to effect His plan
To build the earth into a home for man:
Above the darkness, Wisdom lifts a light
That ends the era of primeval night.
From chaos, order, aims and laws emerge
That fill creation with a righteous urge.
The soil vibrates with joy to heed the call
To yield an ample store to nourish all.

For love of man and with design discreet,
God leaves the human realm still incomplete,
Man's skill to prove and faith in self to test,
By changing what is good into the best.
God offers Wisdom choice of finest place
From which to view the scene and help the race
Approach in course of time the highest goal.
Then Wisdom picks the valiant woman's soul.

SARAH

"I will bless her and she shall be a mother of nations."

Genesis 7:16

A treasury of precious gems, a tree
Of luscious fruits, a veritable sea
From which the whole of life draws sustenance,
Such is the Jewish home where mother's glance
Imparts to her beloved aims sublime
And gilds each day with glow of endless time.
The home is source and center of all bliss,
Since life itself stems from a mother's kiss.

JOCHEBED

"And the woman took the child and nursed it."   Exodus 2:9

The prophecies that linger through the years,
The poetry that glistens in our tears,
The laws by which security is wrought
Are first conceived within a mother's thought.
Heroic deeds that glorify a place,
The prayers and hopes that sanctify a race,
Through credited to man's consummate art,
Are plain mutations of a mother's heart.

MIRIAM

"His sister stood afar off to know what would be done to him."
Exodus 2:4

The spirit is the essence of all life:
The soul behind the plow, the loom, the knife,
The genius in the stone, the flax, the clay
Give worth to work and meaning to a day.
The wealth of all the ages is a seed
Which tender infants carry, that may lead,
If guarded, goaded, guided with all care,
To gladsome victories and virtues rare.

DEBORAH

"The stars in their courses fought against Sisera." Judges 5:20

There is no risk in righteousness, no loss
In price that righteous peace demands, no dross
In creed that teaches man a simple way
To love and live for more than just a day.
If thought and will unite, a single hour
Includes the law of life and nature's power.
When he acquires a taste and will for good,
Man helps God build a cosmic brotherhood.

RUTH

"Entreat me not to leave thee."   Ruth 1:16

The planet teems with treasures manifold,
A magic force the air and waters hold,
But hidden they remain, by God's decree,
Till human love and purpose set them free.
In heart of man, God plants His greatest gift
A dream, a hope, a will, a plan to lift
The whole of life unto the heights above
When moved and guided and sustained by love.

HANNAH

"For not by strength shall man prevail."   I Samuel 2:9

The humble and obscure become the great,
The hungry and the poor whose helpless state
The proud and violent would grind to dust,
Arise to glory, if in God they trust.
Potential good and distant hopes appear
As present facts, when Heaven hovers near.
Man climbs the noblest peaks, strong, high and fair,
Through reverence of God and fervent prayer.

ESTHER

"If I perish, I perish."   Esther 4:16

The life that is not shared, the hand and heart
That shun companionship and keep apart
From scenes o'er which want, woe and sorrows flit,
Is equal to a human counterfeit.
The heart that loves, the voice that thrills a race,
The hand that guards a land must first efface
All fears and doubts, all thoughts of self and gain.
To further human rights and reason's reign.

The great Creator's plan mankind must learn;
To cheer the sick, no lowly brother spurn,
To guard and teach the young, the blind to lead,
To love and heed the truth, good-will to speed,
To grace the Shrine and comfort the opprest,
To sanctify the home with Sabbath rest.
While hands thus learn to work and hearts to pray,
Our earth will welcome Wisdom's perfect sway.

Long may good women seek such ways of life
That conquer want, defeat disease and strife;
Each heart a shrine, a temple in each home,
God's Presence felt wherever man may roam.
May Jewish women guard the world from shame,
And win for Sons of Jacob lasting fame.
And hail the women of dear Jeshurun
Whose deeds each day grow brighter 'neath the sun.

THE SEPULCHRE OF MOSES

"No man knoweth of his sepulchre unto this day."

Deuteronomy 34:6

Resplendent and enduring is the place
Where greatest soul on earth will lie at rest;
No mound, built by the sweat of the opprest;
No precious gems that bear the clearest trace
Of slavish tears and toil, and king's disgrace;
No morbid incantations, to suggest
The monumental tomb to hold the blest,
Whose life and work shine through man's upturned face.

Wherever urge to righteousness is found
And great decisions ripen in the mind,
When law and peace entrance mankind,
And freedom and democracy abound,
Mankind will build the perfect shrine
To Moses, Messenger of the Divine.

THE COAT OF MANY COLORS

"For He hath clothed me with the garments of salvation."
Isaiah 61:10

God made the gorgeous robe that Joseph wore:
No human hand possessed the perfect skill
To weave the cloth and blend the colors till
The robe excelled the best in fashion's store.
The father who bestowed the gift knew more
Than jealous brothers, that a hero's will,
And dreamer's zeal God's purpose to fulfill,
Gave Joseph rights which selfish men abhor.

God makes a robe for every child of earth
Whose visions sparkle with a cosmic gleam;
Whose services and aspirations seem
To weave a fabric of celestial worth.
On measurements of merit God decreed
Man's robe reflects the pattern of his deed.

42

NO MAN CAN SEE GOD'S FACE

"Thou canst not see My face, for man shall not see Me and live."
Exodus 33:20

No man can see God's face, without the urge
To steer his life by rules of righteousness.
Man's conscience is a derelict, unless
His mind and moods, his heart and wishes merge
With the resistless and majestic surge
Of truth and faith that move toward holiness.
The cynic's slurs and flings at Godliness
Evaporate in time's relentless purge.

God's face shines clearest on man's noblest works:
Wherever order rules and good-will reigns;
Whenever justice wins and peace obtains;
Within all simple things, His goodness lurks.
With each advance above the scale of clod,
Man feels the glow of God's approving nod.

GIVE ME A FRIEND

"Give me a friend or let me die."   The Talmud

Like sunshine calling flowers from a seed,
A friendly smile inspires our latent dreams.
Each sympathetic glance enkindles beams
That energize a wish into a deed.
A gentle hand oft plucks a mental weed
And charts a course to optimistic themes.
When kindred souls unite in faith, it seems,
A taste of Heaven on earth is guaranteed.

Our life exhibits one superb design
That links our destiny to the Divine:
To practice the good-will which we profess,
To use God's gifts for human benefit,
To love the true and fair, which make men fit
For peaceful ways and lasting happiness.

OUR LINK TO GOD

To our young-old friends.

"The hoary head is a crown of glory."   Proverbs 16:31

Just as you are to-day,
Unharmed by fleeting years,
Unflinching in life's fray,
And calm despite the tears;

Just as you are to-day
With wrinkled brows and forms
That bend, and hair turned gray
From facing bitter storms;

Just as you are to-day
Unmoved by follies' flare,
Unknown in vice's way,
Of malice unaware;

Just as you are to-day,
With friendship's golden glow,
With lips that gladly pray,
And love on all bestow;

Just as you are to-day,
With faith in truth serene,
With spirits always gay,
And hope for others keen;

Just as you are to-day,
With duty clear and strong,
And conscience holding sway,
Your lives sing like a song.

Just as you are to-day
You have our praise and love;
Forever you must stay,
Our link to God above.

WHAT MEAN THESE THINGS?

"Know ye not what these things mean? Tell them".
Ezekiel 17:12

Your post card route for Richmond tour
Gave me delight, you may be sure;
But keener joy, I say with pride,
Will be my lot, with you as guide.

No print conveys the ardent tones
That animate historic stones:
No type can equal sparkling eyes
Describing fair Virginia skies.

The grandest pictures seem quite pale
Until a heart relates the tale
That lifts the past above the fog
That settles on a catalogue.

A book, a clock, or anything
Depends upon the soul we bring
To grasp the secrets of the hours
That make the minutes bloom with flowers.

To fix a scene in memory,
There's need of personality,
With gesture to accentuate,
Or silently to illustrate

The triumphs of the days agone,
Or glories of the coming dawn.
To scan the past with sympathy
Assures us future ecstasy.

Your cards display a tiny part
Of Richmond's rare and varied art—
Enough to make me realize
What treats await my ears and eyes,

When "On to Richmond" for a day
In peace and joy, I turn my way,
Virginia's treasures to review
And youthful friendship to renew.

IV

THE ROMANCE OF THE CALENDAR

COUNTING TIME

"So teach us to number our days."   Psalms 90:12

With each increase in years,
May we decrease our fears;
As labors lose in length
May work we do gain strength;

May joys we count on earth
Enhance the spirit's worth
And forge, through love of man,
A link to God's great plan;

Let's look above the dust
For wealth that will not rust
And give a selfless hue
To glory we pursue.

All speed we must efface
To reach our proper place;
This law up to the end:
Truth, right, and peace defend.

OUR SPIRITUAL CALENDAR

"We bring our years to an end as a tale that is told."

Psalms 90:9

Sixty smiles a minute
Brighten every hour.
One whole day of effort
Kindles moral power.

Seven days of gladness
Speed the week along.
Four swift weeks of service
Turn dull months to song.

Twelve full months of duty
Glorify the year.
Four-score years of virtue
Bring the Heavens near.

LIFE, LIBERTY AND PURSUIT
OF HAPPINESS

"Pray for the peace of the city . . . for in the peace thereof
  shall ye have peace."   Jeremiah 29:7

From day of birth to death we must depend
On laws and usages with which to blend
Our wisdom, wish and will to safeguard health,
Protect our homes and schools, indeed all wealth.
If joined with fellowmen, we may attain
The mood, the motives and the means to gain
The life, the liberty and happiness,
As passport to the realm of righteousness.
Life loses drudgery, despair and fear,
When soul in prayer conceives God's Presence near.
The dream of liberty evolves to fact,
When conscience stirs the will and molds man's act.
With happiness, no blessing can compare,
If work embraces love and gains mean "share."
Ideals and hopes, offsetting doubts and fears,
Forecast new blessings through the coming years.

BIRTHDAY GREETINGS

"And Moses was a hundred and twenty years old when he
died; his eye was not dim, nor his natural force abated."

Deuteronomy 34:7

A birthday is a hapless date
Unless we learn to dedicate
The strength and skill that we possess
To further human happiness.

Our truest joys stem from the mind
That knows the sorrows of mankind
And counts our wealth by what we give;
Our worth by height on which we live.

These final truths we soon must learn:
The false to hate, the crude to spurn,
The good to seek and God revere
To make our hopes bear fruit all year.

THE NINETIETH YEAR

To B'Nai Jeshurun on the 90th year.

"Ask thy father, and he will declare unto thee, thine elders and they will tell thee." Deuteronomy 32:7

Blow the Shofar in Triumph, in jubilant song raise the voice:
Ninety years of blest service to God gives good cause to rejoice.
Above wealth and position, beyond the rewards of a day,
In pursuit of the treasures and joys that can never decay.

Jewish leaders, like brave pioneers in each era and clime,
Everyone bringing gifts, built our Temple, with vision sublime,
Spreading light in the homes, kindling hope in the hearts, of the true,
Holding firm, for the good of all men, the high faith of the Jew.
Unto us, now beset by confusion and turmoil and strife,
Reading history right, as recorded in Torah and life,
Unto us, from the past comes a message our souls clearly hear:
"Never doubt, God gives strength to His people to banish all fear."

NEW YEAR GREETING

"The Lord lift up His countenance upon thee, and give thee
peace!"   Numbers 6:26

May God's most precious gifts in ample shares
Be ours, for private wants and home affairs;
For Temple work and philanthropic need;
For civic aims, without regard to creed;
For plans and preparations, this New Year,
To see the dawn of world-wide peace appear.

FOR PEACE, BEAUTY AND RECTITUDE

"Oh Lord, our God, how glorious is Thy Name in all the
earth."   Psalms 8:10

In Taormina, Heaven's artistry
Designed from nature's forms a perfect scene,
With gorgeous peaks and trees, with sea serene,
A climate mild, and such fertility,
The flowers with entrancing harmony
Portray the truths great prophets have foreseen:
Man's life and laws must forge a link between
Our earth and God in loving unity.

From choice and logic of this attitude,
Man never can recede. A kindly fate
Supplies enough to build on earth a state
Of peace, of beauty and of rectitude,
If we but share in God's creative plan,
To treat each neighbor as a fellow-man.

ATONEMENT DAY

GOD as HEALER

"Heal me, O GOD, and I shall be healed."   Jeremiah 17:14

As patients, eager to be rid of ills,
Appeal to a physician for relief,
We flock to Thee, O God, with firm belief,
That Thou Alone canst mend our broken wills.

Our minds are dull from enervating schemes;
Our hearts are faint from poisonous desires;
Our souls are scorched by raging inner fires;
And baseless fears enfeeble our best dreams.

As penitents, we now return, O God,
To reaffirm our Faith in Thee. We feel
Thy presence as a precious balm to heal
And bless our lives with Thy forgiving nod.

"A CLEAN HEART AND A STEADFAST SPIRIT"

"Create in me a clean heart, O God,
And renew a steadfast spirit within me."   Psalms 51:12

I

To cleanse the soul of all idolatries:
Review the follies and vulgarities,
The quarrels, hates, feuds, plots and sophistries;
Recall the envies, guiles and vanities;
Pin-point ingratitudes and bigotries,
Which plague all those who fail to itemize
Life's shades and shadows that they satirize.

II

Judge facts and fictions with sincerity:
Compare intent with deed; integrity
With fraud; cite lust at war with chastity;
Pit avarice against philanthropy,
And note, most gratefully, how destiny
Selects the true and brave to eulogize,
And marks the arrogant to penalize.

III

Our joys are fruits which truth and courage yield;
Our agonies are scars of hopes congealed.
If faith in God with love of man be sealed,
And conscience master vice in every field,
Resplendent happiness will be revealed.
Be wise, no further need to theorize;
Pursue the good and win life's noblest prize.

COMMUNION WITH NATURE

"To him who in the love of nature holds communion with
her visible forms, she speaks a various language."

William Cullen Bryant

"Give ear, ye Heavens, and I will speak;
And let the earth hear the words of my mouth."

Deuteronomy 32:1

From the scenes which kind nature displays
In the skies, at the shore, in the ways
Of the woods, the rapt soul, without strain
Leaps the earth to the spirit's domain.

Every sound, every move, every hue
That the eye or the ear ever knew,
Is a missive of import divine,
With a meaning for man in each line.

There is music in fields of ripe grains,
Which, transmuted in sensitive brains,
Fills the world with melodious airs
To soothe life's snarling moods and sharp cares.

The soft beauty the gardens enfold
Reshapes life, to resemble the mold
Of the Artist whose image impressed
On an atom of earth makes it blest.

There is joy in the smile of the brook
Which true lovers attest in their looks,
As their fates blend in love's ecstasy,
Like the currents that merge with the sea.

There is hope in the fruit of the tree,
Which the wise of the earth plainly see,
As they plant great ideals in the youth
For the future's rich harvest of truth.

As recorded in medical lore,
There is health in the mine's common ore,
To help surgeons, with sanctified steel,
To restore to the body its weal.

With the power imbedded in oil
Grievous strain is extracted from toil,
Giving dwellers on earth ample time
To plan life on a plane more sublime.

The swift flight of the eagle through space,
Unsurpassed in its rhythmical grace,
Offers poet a wing for his muse
And a highway his fancy to choose.

When the sun gilds the clouds in the west,
It bids mortals, with troubles opprest
"Kindle wisdom and courage and trust
To illumine earth's darkness and dust."

When the earth and the sky join with man
To embody the Heavenly plan,
We may look to the soul or the sod
And decipher some message from God.

THE LOVE AND PRACTICE OF SERVICE

"The stranger did not lodge in the street;
My doors I opened to the roadside."   Job 31:32

To Travelers Aid

If I were asked to summarize
The qualities which all should prize
That earn for dwellers on this earth
The right to claim surpassing worth;

In justice I would itemize
And with elation publicize,
Wherever in this land I go,
The virtues of a Board I know.

In Travelers Aid I recognize
Our city's aim to organize
The law and love of helpfulness
To every traveler in distress.

In every word you vocalize,
In every act you formalize
The best of counsel to the meek
And prompt assistance to the weak.

Real fellowship you dramatize,
So that the weary realize,
When they must trudge life's darker ways,
You open doors to brighter days.

A better bard should poetize
You aims and skills that energize
The timid, stranded, faint, forlorn
To firmer steps and faith reborn.

A MODERN ESTHER—PURIM

"Who knoweth whether thou art not come to Royal Estate for
   such a time as this?"   Esther 4:14

To Theresa Grotta.

The age and place earn leaders that man needs:
Heav'n knows the fittest time for souls whose deeds
Enrich eternity, to come to birth.
Ripe fruits of faith and love they bring to earth,
Each harvest better than the last in worth.
Such was the noble Esther of Shushan,
A loyal Jewess, upright, brave, serene.

God sent to serve our time another Queen,
Revered by poor and weak who learned to lean
On her strong nature for support. Her zeal
To raise religion and our country's weal
Translates a mind and heart bereft of fears.
A soul like hers we need for endless years.

THE SEAT OF ELIJAH

" 'Come now, and let us reason together,' Saith the LORD."
Isaiah 1:18

Elijah surely takes his seat to-night,
As honor guest at banquet most unique.
The feast is spread on every plain and peak
Wherever Jews might tarry from their flight.
The globe has never known a rarer sight,
An old but virile people, confident but meek,
Who live the world's best story, come to seek
God's help to end on earth an endless night.

He speaks, unseen, but every one can hear:
"These symbols clearly illustrate the way
To meet the tyrant and resist decay,
To hate idolatries and God revere.
True peace will come and brotherhood hold sway,
When men know God and His commands obey."

THE OPEN DOOR

"That the King of Glory may come in."   Psalms 24:9

Unlock the door and let the festive light
With challenging and meaningful brilliance
Illumine foes obsessed with ignorance,
And shame the fiends who seek our death this night.
Invite them to our feast, perhaps the sight
Of bounties to be shared and just a glance
At group at prayer for liberty's advance
Will lead us all in friendship to unite.

Beware the yellow badge that gives the hues
Of fears and degradations of our foes.
The ghetto walls with their attendant woes
Demoralize the builders more than Jews.
The open door most vividly explains,
Good-will to Jews will yield the world great gains.

OUR TRAFFIC LIGHTS

"Light is sown for the righteous
  And gladness for the upright in heart".   Psalms 97:11

Our highway beacons imitate
God's blessed rainbow in the sky:
Through day and night they illustrate
The laws of life which fools deny.

Concern for others we must show
On highways, sea-ways or in air:
Just how we get to where we go,
Commune with conscience and take care.

To treat the roads like anarchists,
Defying safeguards on our way,
Like brutal, stupid realists,
We sponsor Satan's holiday.

The "Red" light which the signals flash,
Means nothing to the blind machine,
But minds that run the risk to crash
Must share the guilt in tragic scene.

The "Green" light beams with joy, "Advance
With measured and with heedful pace
To give the walker better chance
To reach alive his destined place."

Between the "Green" and "Red," two views
The "Yellow" blinks with clarity:
"Red" warns, "a grave or wreck you choose;
Pick 'Green' and earn serenity."

God offers us a mystic light
To brighten life in our domain:
If wish and will we could unite,
World peace and plenty we would gain.

CONFIRMATION HYMN

'Seek ye the Lord while He may be found."   Isaiah 55:6

Lord our God, Thou art here.

Father, now we hear Thy voice,
Calling us into Thy shrine
To receive Thy love devine.
While our hearts and minds rejoice,
Lord our God, we gladly hear.

Father, be Thou near to give
Thy enduring Law of Truth
That shall sanctify our youth,
Teaching us Thy way to live.
Lord our God, we feel Thee near.

Father, here we pray with zeal:
Keep us always true and pure,
Give us faith that shall endure,
Making Thee our ONE IDEAL.
Lord our God, we see Thee here.

V

THE SPIRITUALITY OF LOVE

GUARD THE HEART

"For out of it are the issues of life."   Proverbs 4:23

The final test is love: the heart decides
What artistry the cunning hand performs;
What rules the fertile mind adopts as norms;
How long and where the restless eye abides.
From loveless hearts and sterile souls God hides
The majesty attending nature's forms.
Love magnifies the good, the crude reforms,
And to the heights of fame the humble guides.

The heart that beats in rhythm with the tides
And hears the loving whisperings of God;
The heart that breaks the shackles of the sod
And weeds from fellowmen dank fears and prides;
The heart that finds the trail to lasting good,
Assures the reign of peace and brotherhood.

LOVE IS THE FRUIT OF INNOCENCE

"Thou shalt not hate thy brother in thy heart".

Leviticus 19:17

He does not love who fails to feel a thrill
To see another's cheek flush with the glow
Of deep emotion, on whose soul the flow
Of sentiment acts like a blasting chill.
He cannot love, nor know his loss whose will
Is curved by thought of self; whose aims range low
Upon the earth; whose sympathies are slow
To give response, nor all his being fill.

Love is the luscious fruit of innocence,
The truest, best account man has to give
Of all his work and how he hopes to live,
The crowning joy of his experience.
Profound his love and nobly passionate,
Whose life is true and simple, calm and great.

THE ESSENCE OF TRUE LOVE

"Let not kindness and truth forsake thee. So shalt thou find
grace and good favor In the sight of God and man."

Proverbs 3:4

I cannot give thee love most men admire:
A worship of thy face and form, lip praise
Of less than what thou art. Beyond thy gaze
My senses catch a gleam of Heaven's fire.
Thy tongue drops sweeter honey than the lyre
Of gifted poet; thy graceful tripping sprays
The fields with flowers, and in thy smile the rays
Of virtue shine with magic to inspire.

To me thine eyes, thy voice and all thy grace
Are but the shadows dim of what thou art.
I love thy soul, its tenderness; thy heart,
Its calm; thy mind, with truth in its embrace.
Without thee, pain and stumbling through the night:
Supremest joy that God made thee my light.

THANKS FOR A BOOK

"Thou shalt meditate therein day and night."   Joshua 1:8

I love a book that brings so near a soul
That throbs in words and vibrates in a dream;
That shines in argument and glows with gleam;
Which beckons to the author's distant goal.

The book is doubly blessed with love of friends;
The print, the paragraphs and every page
Reflect augmented lustre, and the sage
Enjoys the shelter of my choice book ends.

IN DEEPEST GRATITUDE

"I shall not die, but live to declare the works of the Lord".
Psalms 118:17

To my dear ones and friends to whom thanks are now due,
From the depths of my heart I am pleased to send you
At least hints of the help with which to fight pain,
That you gave me, with hope of our meeting again.
I am thankful for wishes my health to restore;
For the gifts and attentions which made a fine score;
For the letters and cards that gladdened each day.
With prescriptions and plans to drive illness away;
For the surgeon's great skill and the nurses' kind care,
Which succeeded in making pain easy to bear.
Now God's Presence seems nearer than ever before.
Life's deep meaning is clearer than seen heretofore.
You are dearer now, too, so a favor I ask—
Let's reduce the world's pains as our challenging task.

OUR PERFECT HOME IN LOVER'S LANE

"For love is strong as death."　　　　Song of Songs 8:6

You are my own, Sweetheart, by rightful claim:
Love makes your heart my home and resting place;
Love folds your arms, at best, in my embrace,
And shapes your tongue and lips to breathe my name.
Your smile of welcome glows to mystic flame
With charm to beautify your lovely face.
Love joins our search, through all of life, for trace
Of the Divine, within our mortal frame.

Like castle walls, these arms of mine shall form
Your home. My breast, against life's storms, your shield;
My face, your shade, when summer sears the field;
When winter blows, my breath shall keep you warm.
With love supreme, and life from God we gain,
Our perfect home we'll build in Lover's Lane.

A PART OF ME

I

The skies' expanse
And wealth of earth
Give me the chance
To hint of worth
You are to me.
I cite the sea,
Its mighty force
And majesty,
To join our course
With destiny.

II

The speed of light
Is far too slow
To equal flight
At which I go
To where you are.
Like lustrous star,
With piercing ray,
Through time and space
To show the way
You found the place

III

To be so near,
Through day and night,
With image clear
And spirit bright
Deep in my heart.
No secret art
To do this feat.
Here is the key;
Good made you, Sweet,
A part of me.

LOVE'S MAGICAL POWERS

Many years after these pretty flowers
Counting time by the onrushing hours
Shall become but a sweet memory,
Your devotion and charm, like spring showers
Will endow you with magical powers
To crown life with true love's ecstasy.

COMING HOME

"Grow old along with me! The best is yet to be, The last of life for which the first was made."   Browning

At last, Sweetheart, I'm coming home to rest,
To guard and guide and gladden you,
To thank our God and nature too
For love and life which make us truly blest.

I'm coming home, Sweetheart, with pride to show,
By word and deed, by aim and thought,
What precious boons our love has wrought
To give our path through life its golden glow.

I'm coming home, Sweetheart, for your sweet kiss,
To brighten cares and heighten health,
To count the vastness of our wealth,
In terms of boundless faith and endless bliss.

I'm coming home, Sweetheart, with you to stay,
Love's grandest law to illustrate,
How you and I approximate,
In soul and looks, while love holds right of way.

VI

THE BLESSINGS OF DUTY

LOYALTY

"Iron sharpeneth iron; so a man sharpeneth the countenance
of his friend."   Proverbs 27:17

I need the precious traits I find in you,
To raise my best to higher quality.
For woe or genuine felicity,
My choice of word or deed or work I do,
Reflects the darker or the brighter hue
Of your convictions and activity.
The high or low of your integrity
Gives to my rise or fall the clearest clue.

Intangible connections make us one:
The eye, the hand, the voice exert a spell
On each of us, for good or ill, to tell
How right and peace and love can best be won.
Like sun evoking beauty from the earth,
Your soul inspires mine to riper worth.

SERENITY

"Great peace have they who love Thy Law, O LORD."

Psalms 119:165

Until the end, I shall not cease to pray
That Thou, O GOD, shalt be my only Guide.
Time was, when eagerness to serve and pride
Of work and name allured me to the fray.
A moment came when wisdom showed the way,
To climb life's higher peaks, with measured stride
And tested aims that lift above the tide
Of glamor, greed and guile that rule our day.

I know and love and live the law of right
Which never fails to yield a healing balm
For stings and blows of doubts and fears. Blest calm
It brings, with hope and confidence, so bright,
Illusions fade and pure ideals shine clear.
My plea, O GOD, is proof that Thou dost hear.

GOD'S HELP

"My help cometh from the Lord, Who made Heaven and
  earth."   Psalms 121:2

I lift mine eyes to the eternal hills
Whose majesty dissolves my spirit's scars,
Produced by conflicts on the plain. The bars
The senses raise between the soul and thrills
Of earth's distractions, fall, as limpid rills
Attune me to a hopeful view. The stars
Subdue my fretful mood and nothing mars
My Faith that God the whole creation fills.

For conflicts and confusions on the plain,
We need the meditations of the heights:
The shadows in the valley take their flight,
If insight of the hills we can retain.
God shaped the peaks and plains in unity
And bids us use them in true harmony.

BE FIRM THROUGH THE YEARS

The lone pine.

The lone pine, undismayed by the storms
On the heights, all its roots taking forms
Of the rocks, like a sentinel stands,
And with warrant prophetic, commands:

"Sons of earth, face the winds, have no fears
To aim high and be firm through the years.
Whether lofty or lowly on earth,
What you are, where you are, shows your worth."

HUMAN FLOWERS

"And the desert shall rejoice, and blossom as the rose."

Isaiah 35:1

To Rotary.

A rose is nature's suitable reply
To all who question will of the Divine,
Directing sun and season to apply
Their purest gifts for flower superfine.

With roots sunk deep and strong within the heart
The seeds of friendship yield their human flowers
That give a glimpse of Heaven and impart
To mortals lasting joys and noble powers.

If I might be a cog on Friendship's wheel
And turn with Rotary each word and deed
To civic righteousness and human weal,
I'd have the skill and strength for every need.

SOME KEYS TO SUCCESS

"The Lord will open unto thee His good treasure . . .
to bless all the work of thy hand."   Deuteronomy 28:12

Reflections on keys.

A key is just a symbol
Of values we appraise:
A ring, a watch, a thimble
That tell of by-gone days.

Perhaps a child's attire,
A book or strand of hair,
Are estimated higher
Than gold and gems most rare.

But more than locks are needed
A treasure to protect,
When precepts go unheeded
And men lose self-respect.

Unsafe is any treasure
Which only money buys:
There must be in life's measure
True hearts and laughing eyes.

With honor comes assurance,
Denied mere locks and chains,
To guarantee endurance
Of human hopes and gains.

We'll find that every product
Will serve a worthy use
And nothing in man's conduct
Will tolerate abuse.

No gendarme blocks the entry
To virtue's ample store;
No need to place a sentry
To picket friendship's door.

No gun presents resistance,
When truth and peace we speak;
All nature beams assistance,
If right we bravely seek.

No time-lock sets the hour
To limit what we learn:
On earth there is no power
To thwart the joys we earn.

We greatly gain by giving
And climb as we aspire:
We reach the peak of living
On height of heart's desire.

A cosmic radiation,
Enveloping the soul,
Unlocks the inspiration
For man's immortal role.

VII

THE INSPIRATIONS OF MEMORY AND HOPE

MEMORY AND HOPE

"I will make all My goodness pass before thee." Exodus 33:19

From moments, not from years, our mold is cast,
Which bears the impress of our lives. Like soil
That yields delicious foods, rewarding toil
With patience and with skill applied, the past
Invites us to a bounteous repast.
From woes, the pains are peeled; from sharp turmoil
Is drained its bitter acid, lest we spoil
Our taste for good that lingers to the last.

Above the boon of memory is hope
Which lifts the curtain of the coming years
On gorgeous scenes. Through our attendant tears,
The future rainbows shine, and viture's scope
Becomes so clear and positive we feel
To-day our visions of the good are real.

A BOOK, A FRIEND, AND GOD

"I offer thee three things."   I Chronicles 21:10

Three blessings I implore of destiny
To beautify dull days with hopeful dreams,
And brighten weary nights with steady gleams,
To speed my journey to felicity:

A *Book*, to illustrate the planet's wing
and teach a comradeship with birds and trees;
To humanize events, from which like bees,
I learn to sip the sweet in everything.

A *Friend*, to share the joys of sound and sight
And make all blessings real; to turn the pains
Of time's frustrations into moral gains,
While lifting common goals to Heaven's height.

And God, Who tunes the soul to ecstasy
To find the proofs of world-wide brotherhood
Who cheers and chants the way with signs of good
That open vistas of eternity.

SAFE IN THE ETERNAL HOME

To Sadie.

"The law of kindness is on her tongue."   Proverbs 31:26

How strange, Sweetheart, but how appropriate,
On your last trip, I take you home today!
On all our other journeys, you would say
Such lovely things, my soul to elevate,
About our love, our work, our joy; how fate
Matched soul with soul and smoothed for us the way
To make our years ring like a roundelay.
Beloved, speak of love! Why hesitate?

I hear you better now. Sweet memory.
Without your warmth of voice and glow of eyes,
But with impressive eloquence, supplies
The truths you felt, the hopes you loved, to be
My guide, wherever on this earth I roam,
While you are safe in the Eternal Home.

OUR TEARS REFRESH OUR SOULS

"Let her works praise her in the gates."　　　Proverbs 31:31

I do not weep alone. A multitude,
Sweetheart, laments the passing of your frank,
Sincere and gladsome traits. You scorned the rank
Which wealth bestows and spurned with fortitude
The favors offered by the false and crude.
To barter peace for gold you never sank.
From springs deep in your heart this truth we drank:
Man meets with God on Road to Rectitude.

Our tears, like gentle showers on the earth,
Refresh our souls, creating moral force
To channel grief and gloom into the course
Of courage, calm resolve and higher worth.
Through door of Faith comes true serenity:
You live both here and in Eternity.

SPIRITUAL BREAD

To Bread Loaf Inn.

I revel in a scene of beauty rare,
With friendly peaks and lovely trees and streams
To match the gorgeous skies, while happy dreams
Gain shape and strength and aim in thankful prayer.

Here bread is found by which man truly lives:
The teeming soil to breath and blood is kind;
From fertile souls come thoughts to feed the mind.
Such gifts, each day, to all who seek, God gives.

THY SOUL KEPT FAITH WITH GOD

To Mother Henrietta Cohen Foster.

"A woman that feareth the Lord shall be praised."

Proverbs 31:30

Thy soul kept faith with God. The thrusts of fate
Could never break thy prayerful repose.
The wiles of fortune and life's bitter woes
Were to thy tranquil mind subordinate.
Admidst the whirl of chance and change, thy state
Of changeless faith in the Eternal glows
With wisdom, clear and challenging, and shows
Thy spirit's right to shine among the great.

Thy faith enkindled faith in others. Fools
And foes of God alone were hurt by thee.
Thy intuitions, freed from rigid rules
Of logic to establish clarity,
Revealed the true and good to which the Schools
In time will fix the seal of verity.

THE SPIRIT IN THE WHEELS

"For the spirit of the living creature was in the wheels."
Ezekiel 1:21

The wisdom of the ages shines
From this superlative command
That offers all, on basic lines,
The right of safety in each land.

God's spirit radiated light
Throughout creation's vast expanse,
As pledge and pattern of the height
To which earth's gifts man might enhance.

The "STOP" affords a needed pause
To give humanity a chance
As brothers' keepers and the cause
Of common welfare to advance.

The "LOOK" provides the clear insight,
As shield from death and family pain,
And kindling conscience with the light
Of human joy and nation's gain.

To "LISTEN" trains the wish and will
With habits that reflect ideals,
At every turn, each day, until
Man rules machines the way he feels.

THESE THINGS WE KNOW

"The secret things belong unto the Lord our God; but the things that are revealed belong unto us and to our children for ever."   Deuteronomy 29:28

God planted in the soul of man
The urge to find the secret clue
Of life's adventure, and the plan
To make each worthy dream come true.

Some samples of humanity
Brought rule and role of rectitude:
From whispers of Divinity
Grew logic of infinitude.

"Can man by searching find out God?"
What treasure can compare with Him?
The flower rising from the sod,
Our prayer and praise, but hints of Him.

These things we know—as Architect,
God gave us life to regulate;
A globe with treasures to protect,
And laws of peace to emulate.

The moment we select the right,
And turn from self to self-control,
The quicker evils take their flight
And speed our way to higher goal.

Progression's law God has decreed:
No age, nor art, nor creed, not race
Needs end its growth. We must proceed
With faith and strength, or meet disgrace.

By thanking God for Holy Writ
Whose laws and legends chart the ways
Our forebears chose, may prove we're fit
To guide mankind to brighter days.

OUR SPIRITUAL CLOCK

"I have set before thee life and death, the blessing and the curse; therefore choose life that thou mayest live, thou and thy seed".   Deuteronomy 30:19

"Seven times a day do I prase Thee, because of Thy righteous ordinances".   Psalms 119:164

Through life, time circles everything:
We plant and reap and cook, by time;
We grow and play and think and sing,
To give life sense and aims sublime.

Our clocks serve best, discounting fate:
How tackle chores and catch a train;
Why plan a feast and keep a date
With happiness, our goals explain.

"Think-Act, Grip-Faith, Be-Firm," they chime:
Each word or deed, with thought amiss,
May plunge us into woe or crime,
While faith and firmness echo bliss.

The dial, hands and case of gold
Rate less in watch than works inside;
So mind and heart and soul must mold
Our dealings with the world outside.

A morning prayer exalts the day;
An evening plea brings restful night;
Our food tastes better, if we pray,
And envy, fear and wrath take flight.

Our fervent search for inner peace
We may attain, through endless hours,
If we, with help of God, increase,
Each day, our own creative powers.

Praise God for conscience, as a link
Uniting Heaven and our earth,
Recording all we love and think,
As index of our human worth.

RESUME THE TRAIL

"The Lord will send His angel with thee and prosper thy way."
Genesis 24:40

A conflict, somewhere, always breaks a trail
And stays the zest awaited on the height,
In rest, reflection, and the eager sight
Of peaks whose inspirations never fail.
The soul distills wise counsel; "Do not pale
Before this handicap. I test your right
And will to reach your goal before the night.
Discount this hindrance and resume the trail."

The ways of life, unfailingly, traverse
Uncharted envies, devasting hate,
Tumultuous fears, misread decrees of fate,
To change our goals and chosen roads reverse.
The hazards oft provide the pause we need
To prove our right and duty to proceed.

THE SHORTEST DISTANCE
TO SPIRITUALITY

"O Lord, make Thy way Straight before my face". Psalms 5:9

"Such is the word of the Lord, precept . . . line by
line . . . Here a little, there a little".   Isaiah 28:13

1

Two points in space that we unite
Need straightest line that we can draw
To radiate Creation's Light
And vitalize man's moral law.

2

Alone we stray; apart we waste
Our health and life; we choose detours
To peace and right, and lose the taste
For happiness which love procures.

3

Our thoughts possess a latent urge,
But never reach an orbit's range,
Until mind sharpens mind to merger
The heart and hand in fair exchange.

4

When parents' faith wins child's accord,
The home entreats society
To rid the world of mad discord
That threatens world felicity.

5

Good teachers must have more than rules
And texts to serve our ardent youths
Whose future joys stem from the schools
And fruitful seeds of lasting truths.

6

If ministers with flocks combine
As one to study, serve and pray
To lead the world to the Divine;
Serenity will come to stay.

7

True friendship needs more than a name
To fuse two souls in amity,
Enkindling the ennobling flame
Of mutual integrity.

8

The true, the brave, the wise must win,
Because on God we can rely.
All else is froth, or hate, or sin,
Which God expects us to defy.

9

This is the law of brotherhood
Which every age anew must learn:
Our thought and toil for human good
Will gauge the happiness we earn.

10

In scaling heights at breathless speed
And searching for uncharted space,
Remember, our supremest need:
Keep Faith In God, in every place.